Collins

INTERNATIONAL
PRIMARY
ENGLISH

AF005296

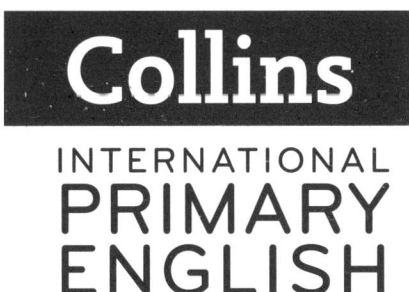

Workbook 4

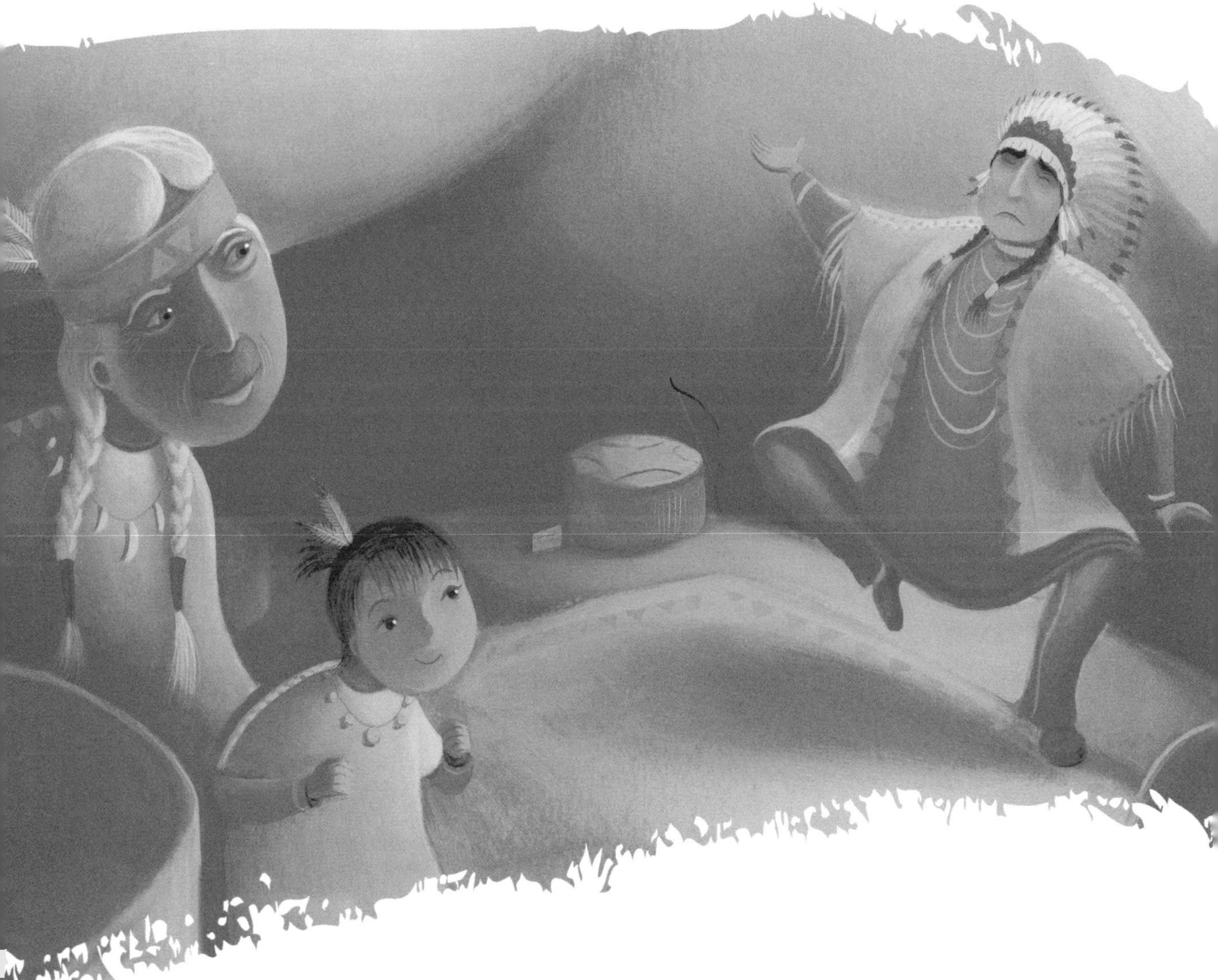

William Collins' dream of knowledge for all began with the publication of his first book in 1819. A self-educated mill worker, he not only enriched millions of lives, but also founded a flourishing publishing house. Today, staying true to this spirit, Collins books are packed with inspiration, innovation and practical expertise. They place you at the centre of a world of possibility and give you exactly what you need to explore it.

Collins. Freedom to teach.

Published by Collins
An imprint of HarperCollins*Publishers*
The News Building
1 London Bridge Street
London SE1 9GF

HarperCollins*Publishers*
Macken House, 39/40 Mayor Street Upper,
Dublin 1, D01 C9W8, Ireland

Browse the complete Collins catalogue at
www.collins.co.uk

© HarperCollins*Publishers* Limited 2021

10 9 8

ISBN 978-0-00-836772-5

All rights reserved. No part of this publication may be reproduced, stored in a retrieval system, or transmitted in any form by any means, electronic, mechanical, photocopying, recording or otherwise, without the prior written permission of the Publisher or a licence permitting restricted copying in the United Kingdom issued by the Copyright Licensing Agency Ltd, 5th Floor, Shackleton House, 4 Battle Bridge Lane, London SE1 2HX.

British Library Cataloguing-in-Publication Data
A catalogue record for this publication is available from the British Library.

Author: Catherine Baker and Daphne Paizee
Series editor: Daphne Paizee
Publisher: Elaine Higgleton
Product developer: Natasha Paul
Project manager: Karen Williams
Development editor: Sonya Newland
Copyeditor: Karen Williams
Proofreader: Catherine Dakin
Cover designer: Gordon MacGilp
Cover illustrator: Richard Johnson
Internal designer and typesetter: Ken Vail Graphic Design Ltd.
Text permissions researcher: Rachel Thorne
Image permissions researcher: Alison Prior
Illustrators: Ken Vail Graphic Design Ltd., Advocate Art, Beehive Illustration and QBS Learning
Production controller: Lyndsey Rogers

Printed in India by Multivista Global Pvt. Ltd.

Text acknowledgements
The publishers gratefully acknowledge the permissions granted to reproduce copyright material in the book. Every effort has been made to contact the holders of copyright material, but if any have been inadvertently overlooked, the Publisher will be pleased to make the necessary arrangements at the first opportunity.

Cover illustration: *The Brave Baby* Reprinted by permission of HarperCollins*Publishers* Ltd © 2004 Malachy Doyle, illustrated by Richard Johnson.

Let's Go To Mars Reprinted by permission of HarperCollins*Publishers* Ltd © 2005 Janice Marriott, illustrated by Mark Ruffle; *The Brave Baby* Reprinted by permission of HarperCollins*Publishers* Ltd © 2004 Malachy Doyle, illustrated by Richard Johnson; *Peter and the Wolf* Reprinted by permission of HarperCollins*Publishers* Ltd © 2007 Diane Redmond, illustrated by John Bendall-Brunello.

We are grateful to the following for permission to reproduce copyright material:

Extracts on p.31 from *Goggle Eyes* by Anne Fine, Penguin, copyright © Anne Fine, 1989. Reproduced with permission of David Higham Associates; and the poem on p.17 "Old Man Ocean" by Russell Hoban published in *The Pedalling Man*, Heinemann, 1991 © The Trustees of the Russell Hoban Trust. Reproduced with permission of David Higham Associates.

Third-party websites, publications and resources referred to in this publication have not been endorsed by Cambridge Assessment International Education.

With thanks to the following teachers and schools for reviewing materials in development: Amanda DuPratt, Shreyaa Dutta Gupta, Sharmila Majumdar, Sushmita Ray and Sukanya Singhal, Calcutta International School; Akash Raut, DSB International School, Mumbai; Melissa Brobst, International School of Budapest; Shalini Reddy, Manthan International School; Taman Rama Intercultural School.

Photo acknowledgements
The publishers wish to thank the following for permission to reproduce photographs. Every effort has been made to trace copyright holders and to obtain their permission for the use of copyright materials. The publishers will gladly receive any information enabling them to rectify any error or omission at the first opportunity.

(t = top, c = centre, b = bottom, r = right, l = left)

p4 stockshoppe/Shutterstock, p6 Lorelyn Medina/Shutterstock, p9 Matthew Cole/Shutterstock, p11 Aliaksei_Z/Shutterstock, p12 Ermolaev Alexander/Shutterstock, p13 John T Takai/Shutterstock, p17 Andrey Yurlov/Shutterstock, p18 Eva Bidiuk/Shutterstock, p19 imageBROKER/Alamy Stock Photo, p20 pzAxe/Shutterstock, p21 VladimirCeresnak/Shutterstock, p27 Matthew Cole/Shutterstock, p28t Eric Isselee/Shutterstock, p28b skylark art/Shutterstock, p29 Lorelyn Medina/Shutterstock, p30 koya979/Shutterstock, p31 stockyimages/Shutterstock, p36 titosart/Shutterstock, p37 Jstone/Shutterstock, p38 Christian Vinces/Shutterstock, p40 Blambca/Shutterstock, p42 humphrey/Shutterstock, p43 Kozyreva Elena/Shutterstock, p53 Anton Brand/Shutterstock, p55 iStock/ThinkStock.

This book contains FSC™ certified paper and other controlled sources to ensure responsible forest management.

For more information visit: www.harpercollins.co.uk/green

Contents

1 Stories of the past page 1

2 Mars: the trip of a lifetime! page 9

3 The power of the sea page 17

4 Other people, other places page 24

5 The only problem is … page 31

6 Making the headlines page 37

7 Inventions page 42

8 Putting on a show page 49

9 Imaginary worlds page 53

1 Stories of the past

Reading Student's Book pages 2–3

1 Reread *Street Child* on pages 2–3 of the Student's Book. What do you think Barnie was thinking as he stared into the fire? Write his thoughts in the thought bubble.

2 What kind of person is Barnie? Fill in the spider diagram with words and phrases to describe him.

What he looks like:

How he talks:

Barnie

What he does:

How he treats Jim:

Four words to describe him:

Verbs   Student's Book page 4

1 Fill in the missing parts of the verb 'to be' in the boxes below.

Present	Past	Future
I am	I _____	I _____
You _____	You were	You will be
She is	He _____	It _____
We _____	We were	We _____
They _____	They _____	They will be

2 Add the correct part of the verb 'to be' to each sentence below.

a **Present:** I _____ the fastest runner in my class.

b **Present:** Amira _____ my sister's best friend.

c **Past:** Dad _____ very good at maths when he _____ my age.

d **Past:** Jon's favourite meal _____ chicken stir-fry.

e **Future:** We _____ at Grandma's house this weekend.

f **Future:** Sahar says she _____ an astronaut when she grows up.

3 Sami is telling his friend what he did last weekend. Write what he is saying. Remember to use the past tense and to use punctuation.

Powerful verbs — Student's Book page 5

1 Underline all the verbs in the sentences below. Then rewrite each sentence, replacing the verbs with more powerful ones.

- Jim <u>walked</u> slowly towards the market.

  Jim plodded slowly towards the market.

  _____

- Bupe looked at Ali.

  _____

- Meera spoke quietly.

  _____

- Stanley ran all the way home.

  _____

- Suresh went upstairs.

  _____

2 Add speech marks to the sentences below. Fill the gaps with interesting words for 'said'.

a "I'm sorry," _____whispered_____ Alice.

b How dare you? _____ Mrs Sangheera.

c It's so exciting! _____ Matthew.

d Have you eaten your breakfast? _____ Mum.

e It's time for school! _____ Ella.

f I've got a sore throat, _____ Rajiv.

g We're going shopping this afternoon, _____ Michael.

h Don't let him hear you, _____ Selma.

i It's bedtime in five minutes, _____ Auntie Bess.

j Stop that at once! _____ Mr Taylor.

Punctuation — Student's Book page 5

1 All the punctuation marks are missing. Write the sentences and add the punctuation. You can use . , ? ! " "

a What do you want for lunch

b I like playing football cricket and tennis

c Look I can see a dragon

d My sister loves going swimming

e Miguel Tom Sam and Kieran are playing volleyball on the beach

f Are we nearly there yet asked Molly

g Look out or you'll crash

2 **Add capital letters to the sentences below. Write the sentences.**

my three best friends are natalia, mindi and mika. we all live in the same street called park street. it's in the middle of the town and quite close to school.

_____

_____

_____

3 **Add commas to the sentences below. Write the sentences.**

a   The kittens' names are Minou Hummel Spot and Snowball.

_____

b   Ahmed's new top has stripes of red green white and blue.

_____

c   You won't tell anyone will you?

_____

d   I ate a samosa a packet of peanuts an apple and a banana.

_____

e   "Now" said Meena slowly. "Let's start again."

_____

4 **Circle the words below that use the apostrophe correctly.**

a   I found Michael's/Michaels'/Micha'els bag.

b   The children's/child'rens/childrens' bedroom was very messy.

c   The girls/girl's/girls' mouths were open in surprise.

d   The dragons'/dragon's/dra'gons/tail was long and scaly.

e   Grandad's/Grandads'/Gran'dads favourite chair is broken.

f   We could hear the sound of the womens'/women's/wom'ens voices.

g   My brothers'/brother's/brothers arm is broken.

h   The boys'/boys/boy's mothers came running.

Spelling and vocabulary — Student's Book page 6

Read the sentences below with –ing and –ed verbs. Draw a circle around the verbs that are spelled correctly. Rewrite the verbs that are spelled incorrectly.

a   Lee is puting his football boots on. _____

b   Carlo cleanned up his room quickly before Mum saw it. _____

c   The old cat is sitting in the sunshine. _____

d   Shh! The baby is sleepping! _____

e   Grandad is digging in the garden. _____

f   I asked if I could have an extra slice of cake. _____

g   Gabriela had a lot of trouble findding her phone charger. _____

h   I've been working hard all day. _____

i   Poppy hoped from one foot to the other impatiently. _____

j   Asif stepped carefully across the thin wooden plank. _____

Reading and writing
Student's Book page 10

1 Read the start of the historical story below. Choose a connective from the box to fill each of the gaps.

> or   because   however   and   because   but

Tom yawned _____ stretched sleepily. It was the start of his first day at Doctor Thomas Barnardo's home for destitute boys. Tom had come to the home the previous evening, _____ he had no food and nowhere to live. He knew that Doctor Barnardo would let him come in, _____ Doctor Barnardo was famous for his kindness to poor children. _____, Tom was nervous this morning. What would life in Doctor Barnardo's home be like? Would he fit in with the other boys _____ would they make fun of him? Tom wanted to stay under the blankets a while longer, _____ he knew that he had to get up and face the day.

2 Write the next paragraph of the story below. You can decide what happens. Use connectives in some of your sentences.

_____
_____
_____
_____
_____

3 Read the sentences below. Write an adjective to fill each gap.

a My baby sister loves her _____, _____ teddy bear.

b Mina has _____ hair and _____ eyes.

c Brandon's mum is very _____.

d I put on my coat because it was a _____ day.

e The monster had fourteen _____ eyes and a hundred _____ teeth.

4 Replace the underlined adjective with a stronger adjective from the box. Write the new sentence.

| tiny | gigantic | freezing | boiling | young | ancient |
| ravenous | disgusting | full | terrifying | enormous | |

a It was <u>cold</u> and Marti's teeth chattered.
_____

b Ella pulled on an <u>old</u> T-shirt and went out to play.
_____

c Jamie was <u>hungry</u>, so he ate his sandwich.
_____

d It was <u>scary</u> being out alone in the dark.
_____

e Mariam saw a <u>small</u> kitten peeping out through the gate.
_____

8

2 Mars: the trip of a lifetime!

Reading Student's Book page 13

Read the facts below about Mars.

a Draw a wavy line under any facts that make Mars sound like a good place to visit.

b Draw a circle round any facts that make Mars sound like a bad place to visit.

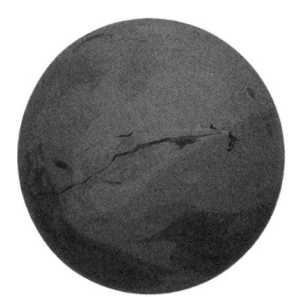

Would you like to go to Mars? Here are some Martian facts to help you make up your mind!

- Mars is Earth's next-door neighbour. Earth is the third planet from the Sun, and Mars is the fourth planet. But, even though they are neighbours in the Solar System, Earth and Mars are still about 225 million kilometres apart. It would take roughly 260 days to get from Earth to Mars.

- Mars is smaller, colder and drier than Earth. The average temperature on Mars is −62°C. That's 62 degrees below freezing, which is colder than Earth's Arctic Circle in the middle of winter!

- Mars is often called the 'Red Planet' because of its red soil. The soil on Mars is red because it is rusty (it contains iron oxide).

- Mars's rusty, dusty soil is very dry indeed. Sometimes there are enormous duststorms on Mars – big enough to cover the whole planet!

- Even though the surface of Mars is so dry, scientists have discovered that there is lots of frozen water under the surface of the planet. This means that if people ever travelled to Mars, they might be able to get the water they need by extracting and melting the ice.

- The air on Mars is mostly carbon dioxide, which is poisonous to humans – so any visitors would definitely need a spacesuit to survive!

- There are lots of interesting things to see on Mars. The massive volcano called Olympus Mons is three times bigger than Everest – and it is probably the biggest volcano in the whole Solar System. There is also an enormous canyon on Mars that is nearly as long as the United States of America is wide! At night, you would see not one, but two moons rising in the sky.

Reading   Student's Book pages 14–16

1 Read the sentences below. Write F at the end of the facts and write O at the end of the opinions.

a Mars would be a really fun place to visit. ☐

b No human beings have ever yet gone to Mars. ☐

c Mars is the fourth planet from the Sun. ☐

d Mars is colder than Earth. ☐

e Life on Earth is a lot more interesting than life on Mars. ☐

f Mars has two moons. ☐

g Nights on Mars are more beautiful than nights on Earth. ☐

h It is too dangerous for humans to visit Mars. ☐

i Humans need spacesuits to protect them if they visit Mars. ☐

j The soil on Mars is a much nicer colour than the soil on Earth. ☐

2 Find an interesting fact about Mars. Write it here.

Persuasive language — Student's Book page 17

1 **Underline the verbs below that make the sentences persuasive.**

a Watch the sunset from your bedroom in the hotel.

b Race across the red sand in a sand yacht.

c Visit Mars this year!

d Don't miss this opportunity to go on an amazing trip.

e Feel the unimaginable power of a Martian duststorm!

2 **Write a persuasive order about each of the things listed below.**

Remember! You are trying to encourage someone to do something.

a go swimming

Come and swim with us!

b help make a meal

_____

c learn to cycle

_____

d eat fruit

_____

e visit Mars

_____

Spelling and vocabulary Student's Book page 18

1 Rewrite the words below adding the prefix *un–* to the start. Then use each *un–* word in a sentence.

a pleasant _____
_____

b kind _____
_____

c happy _____
_____

d seen _____
_____

e used _____
_____

f eaten _____
_____

2 Add the suffix *–able* to the words below.

a use _____   b believe _____

c accept _____   d regret _____

e adore _____   f do _____

g fashion _____ h enjoy _____

3 Choose two of your 'able' words and write a dictionary definition for each of them.

a Word: _____

   Definition: _____

b Word: _____

   Definition: _____

12

Sentence types — Student's Book pages 19–20

Write out the sentences below and add the missing capital letters and punctuation. Write 'O' by the sentences that are orders, 'Q' by the questions and 'S' by the statements.

a i like chocolate biscuits best

b have you seen my football

c come here at once kieran

d why do you always eat the strawberry sweets first

e we wanted to go to the beach with sam and mina because it was so hot

f be careful or you'll wake the baby

g mum says it's bedtime now

h who is the fastest runner in the class

i shut the door

j the monster was taller than a block of flats

Connectives — Student's Book page 22

1 Read the sentences below. Underline the connectives.

Remember!
Some sentences have more than one connective.

a Marta's room was very untidy, **but** Lucas's room was spotless.

b I like to hum under my breath **because** it makes me feel happy, **but** it annoys my sister.

c First you turn left, **and then** you cross the road under the bridge.

d I like chocolate ice cream **and** Maria likes strawberry, **but** neither of us likes vanilla.

e You'll miss the bus to school, **if** you don't hurry up.

f Mr Osei told Jacob off **because** he was late to school **and** he had forgotten his homework.

g **If** you want to be a good footballer, first you need to practise hard, **because** there are lots of skills to learn.

2 Choose from the connectives in the box and use them to write three sentences of your own.

> first   next   then   because   however   also   if

_____

_____

_____

Commas, connectives and tenses   Student's Book page 23

Read the story below. Then answer the questions below and on page 16.

"Josh! Look at that!"

Jamelia pointed to the sky behind her brother's head, and Josh spun round, his mouth open in amazement. Flapping slowly towards them, its leathery black wings stretched wide against the sky, was the most enormous dragon either of them had ever seen.

"What a beauty," whispered Josh, as he looked towards the clump of trees where the dragon was landing. "It's a Salamander Black. Have you got your phone, Jamelia? We've got to get a picture of this, or no one will ever believe it!"

Jamelia fumbled in her backpack, and a shower of objects fell out: an apple core, a torch, a small folding magic wand, a half-eaten chocolate bar and a hair band. However, there was no sign of Jamelia's phone, because she had left it behind on the bus! Jamelia looked up hopelessly, but Josh was already running across the field, and heading straight for the dragon.

a Underline a sentence where there are commas separating items in a list.
b Find all the sentences where commas are used to separate clauses and underline them.
c Draw circles around all the connectives.

d Find and write out a sentence which uses the future tense.

_____

e Find and write out a sentence which uses the past tense.

_____

f Find and write out a sentence which uses the present tense.

_____

g What kind of dragon have the children seen?

_____

h Are the children in the countryside or in the town? How do you know?

_____

_____

i Do you think the children have ever seen a dragon before? Give a reason for your answer.

_____

_____

j What relation is Jamelia to Josh?

_____

_____

k What clues in the story tell us there is something unusual about the children?

_____

_____

l What do you think will happen next?

_____

_____

3 The power of the sea

Reading Student's Book page 27

1 Read the poem below.

> **Old Man Ocean**
>
> **by Russell Hoban**
>
> Old Man Ocean, how do you pound
> Smooth glass rough, rough stones round?
> *Time and the tide and the wild waves rolling.*
> *Night and the wind and the long grey dawn.*
>
> Old Man Ocean, what do you tell?
> What do you sing in the empty shell?
> *Fog and the storm and the long bell tolling,*
> *Bones in the deep and the brave men gone.*

2 Answer the questions.

a Who is the poet talking to?

_____

b Read the first two lines of the poem again. What two things does the poet say that Old Man Ocean is changing?

_____

_____

c Why do you think the last two lines of each verse are in italic print?

_____

_____

d What do you think Old Man Ocean means when he says that he sings about 'bones in the deep and brave men gone'?

e Give an example of alliteration in the poem.

f Write down two words from the poem that rhyme.

Figurative language — Student's Book page 28

1 Read the sentences below and underline the similes.

a The sea is as cold as an iron nail.

b The sun was shining like a bright mirror.

c The tall trees are like ships sailing across the sea.

d The moon rose through the sky as slowly as a butterfly.

e The silver ship glided across the silent sea like a whisper.

f The children were wriggling like tadpoles.

2 Now read the sentences again and circle words with alliteration.

Reading and writing   Student's Book pages 31–32

1 Read the explanation text below.

> **How butter is made**
>
> i) Butter is made from milk. First the cream is separated from the milk. The cream is put into a container and shaken or churned until it gets thick.
>
> ii) As it is churned the cream gets thicker and thicker. It also turns pale yellow. Eventually it turns solid. The solid stuff is butter! There is also some thin liquid left – this is called buttermilk.
>
> iii) The buttermilk is poured away leaving the butter behind.
>
> iv) Sometimes salt is added to the butter before it is shaped into blocks and wrapped up. Then it is ready to be sold.

2 Write the answers to the questions below.

a What do you have to do to the milk before you can make butter?

_____

_____

b The text says that the cream is 'churned'. What does 'churned' mean?

_____

_____

c What is buttermilk?

_____

_____

d At what stage can you add salt?

_____

_____

Verb tenses   Student's Book pages 31–32

Reread the explanation text about making butter on page 19 of this Workbook. Then answer the questions below.

1 Is the explanation text in the past, present or future tense?

2 Underline all the parts of the verb 'to be' in the section below.

> Butter is made from milk. First, the cream is separated from the milk. The cream is put into a container and shaken, or churned, until it gets thick.

3 Write out the section above. Change all the present-tense verbs to past tense.

4 The verbs in the sentences below are wrong. Write out the sentences correctly.

a The boys was playing cricket on the beach.

b Last Wednesday the weather is very hot.

c We am going to the playground after school.

d In the future we was able to live on the Moon.

e I is bringing my little sister with me because Mum and Dad am out shopping.

Adjectives, adverbs and adverbial phrases

Student's Book page 33

1 Read the sentences below. Circle the adjectives. Underline the adverbs and adverbial phrases.

a Jake bravely dived into the deep, green pool.

b Sasha's sister Kia was small, but noisy.

c I looked both ways carefully before crossing the busy road.

d The trees were waving about furiously in the strong wind.

2 Find four adjectives and four adverbs in the word search puzzle below.

f	i	e	r	c	e	l	y	l	q
w	f	q	b	z	f	j	b	o	s
q	b	e	a	u	t	i	f	u	l
k	z	n	j	h	y	c	h	d	e
f	h	o	w	z	f	x	k	l	e
s	t	r	a	n	g	e	w	y	p
x	w	m	h	z	s	c	a	r	i
j	b	o	q	j	q	w	c	q	l
h	q	u	i	c	k	l	y	j	y
b	z	s	c	a	r	y	f	z	k

3 Choose one adjective and one adverb. Write a sentence with each word.

_____

_____

Spelling — Student's Book page 34

1 The words from three different word families have been mixed up. Write the words into the correct spider diagrams.

> really   reappear   reality   darkest   appearance
> realistic   darker   surreal   apparently   disappear
> darkening   appearing   darkness   unreal   darkly

real

appear

dark

2 Look at the words in the 'real' family. Write a sentence using each word. Check you know what each word means first.

_____

_____

_____

_____

_____

3 Fill in the word family for the root word 'play'. Find at least five members of the family.

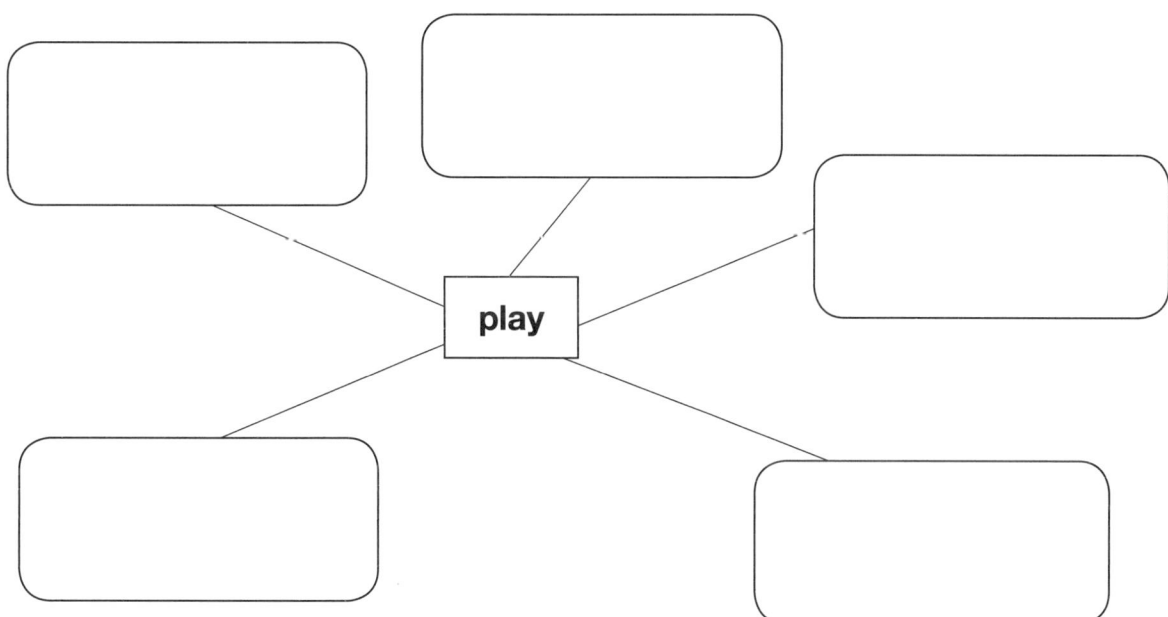

4 Other people, other places

Listening and speaking   Student's Book page 39

1 Think about the story *The Clever Farmer*. Choose one character from the list below.

- the farmer
- the rich man
- Shikorina the cow

Write their name in the middle of the spider diagram. Add words and phrases to describe the character you have chosen.

What the character might look like:	What the character does:

What other people think of the character:	Four words to describe the character:

2 Would you like to meet this character? Give a reason for your answer.

_____
_____
_____

3 **Here is the first paragraph of *The Clever Farmer*.**

   a What clues does it give you about the setting of the story?
   b Underline all the words and phrases that help you to imagine the setting.

Once there was a farmer who had fallen on hard times. His fields were full of dust and stones, his watermelons were all shrivelled up, and worst of all, he had had to get rid of all his cows. All except one, that is. The farmer couldn't bear to part with his last cow. She was the sweetest-natured animal you ever saw, and her name was Shikorina. As long as there was a bite of food in the house, the farmer shared it with Shikorina and they managed to get by, somehow.

4 **Write two sentences to describe the story setting. Make them as detailed and descriptive as you can.**

_____
_____
_____
_____

Reading and writing   Student's Book page 42

1 **Read the story of *Abunuwasi's House* again. Write a different ending for the story.**

_____
_____
_____
_____

2 Read the words in the speech bubbles below. Write the words as direct speech.

Remember!
Use speech punctuation and the speaker's name.

Come back. I only want to play with you.

No thank you! I know what your games are like!

_____
_____
_____
_____
_____
_____
_____

Apostrophes and quantifiers   Student's Book page 43

1 Add the missing apostrophes to the sentences below.

a   Jakes toys were all over the floor.

b   The childrens faces were covered in chocolate.

c   The dragons cave was dark and damp. (Only one dragon.)

d   Maras job was to fill up her pet hamsters water bowl. (More than one hamster.)

e   The girls bicycles had flat tyres. (More than one girl.)

f   Eshe looked everywhere for Sams lost bear.

g   The mens changing room was very crowded.

h   We scattered the chickens food all over the yard. (More than one chicken)

i   The rabbits leg was broken.

j   My mobile phones battery is dead.

2 **Circle the best word to complete each sentence.**

a He (either/or) had to live upstairs or downstairs. He couldn't decide.

b After school I'll meet with (some/none) of my friends and we'll play a game.

c She had (all/some) the money she needed to start a new life.

d (Both/All) Liam and Shelagh have older sisters.

e Abunuwasi and the merchant (both/either) lived in the same house for a while.

f Abunuwasi asked (some/all) strong men to come with him to visit the merchant.

Writing   Student's Book page 47

1 **Underline the adjectives in the sentences below. Then write the sentences out. Change each adjective into a stronger one.**

Kamila was <u>happy</u> to see her friends.

<u>Kamila was delighted to see her friends.</u>

a There was a small kitten asleep in the chair.

_____

b A large dinosaur suddenly burst out of the wood.

_____

c Mandla was cold so he put on his coat.

_____

d We enjoyed our ice creams because it was a hot day.

_____

e The old giant was angry.

_____

2 Add an adverb to each sentence below. Then write the new sentence on the line.

a   Jack skipped home.

_____

b   The giant roared at us.

_____

c   Mum hugged me.

_____

d   I ran downstairs.

_____

e   An owl flew past.

_____

Spelling Student's Book pages 47–48

1 How many syllables are in each of the words below? Write the number next to each word.

a   happily _____   b   correct _____
c   kicking _____   d   somebody _____
e   underneath _____   f   beautiful _____

2 One word in each of the sentences below is spelled incorrectly. Write the word correctly at the end of the line.

a   Sumbody must have taken my book. _____
b   I feel happy wenever I hear that song. _____
c   My fayvorite meal is pizza. _____
d   Evryone makes mistakes sometimes. _____
e   It's a byootiful day. _____

3 **The wrong homophones have been used in the sentences below. Cross out the wrong homophones and write the correct spelling above.**

a   These are my new friends. There from South America.

b   I've got two much homework too do.

c   Adwin is good at reading and righting.

d   I wood love to go swimming.

e   I have bean to Kuala Lumpur. Have you ever been their?

f   Dad is knot hear this evening.

4 **Write a sentence using each of the homophone words correctly.**

a   seen _____

b   scene _____

c   sum _____

d   there _____

e   here _____

f   hear _____

Verb tenses   Student's Book page 48

1 **Write each sentence below in the past tense.**

a   I am excited because it is my turn to go down the water slide.
_____

b   Priti is wearing her best blue sari.
_____

c   We are walking into town.
_____

d   Michael and Ruben are arguing again.
_____

2 Write all the past tense sentences below in the future tense. Write all the future tense sentences in the past tense.

    a Dad was in New York.

    b I will be nine on Saturday.

    c Sabah and Emily will be the winners.

    d We were happy to see Grandma.

3 Change the sentences below from the present tense to the past tense. Some of the verbs are irregular.

    a Mum becomes very cross when we get mud on the carpet.

    b I write my name carefully.

    c The dragon flies over the rooftops.

    d Ruth and Jacob come swimming with us.

    e A large parcel stands in the corner of the room.

5 The only problem is ...

Reading Student's Book pages 53–54

Remember!
Not every sentence has an adjective and some have more than one adjective.

1 Read the sentences below from *Meeting Mr Faulkner*. Underline the adjectives and draw a circle round the verbs.

a   He did have the most enormous box of chocolates tucked under one arm.

b   I sidled out of the shadow.

c   They were those rich, dark, expensive, chocolate-coated cream mints.

d   Jude rushed upstairs, clutching her booty to her chest.

e   Jude came thundering downstairs.

f   He tipped the enraptured Floss into Jude's arms, and ambled past me with a nod.

2 Draw a line to link the verbs that are similar in meaning. Draw a circle round the verb that is the strongest.

walk   chatter
sprint   slump
gobble   eat
giggle   run
smile   plod
sit   laugh
talk   grin

Adverbs — Student's Book page 55

1 Underline the adverbs in the sentences below. Draw a circle round the verb that goes with each adverb.

a I stupidly put the ice cream in the oven instead of in the freezer.

b Jonathan jumped around excitedly.

c Samira looked sadly out of the window.

d "Yippee! We've got my favourite food for dinner!" yelped Mica delightedly.

e Rafiq clumsily dropped his glass on the floor.

f Miserably, Santi plodded home.

g "Never mind, Michael," Ella whispered softly.

h Mr Wong loudly shouted, "Go back to your seats at once!"

2 Write the sentences below. Add an adverb to each sentence.

a I trod on my best pen and broke it.

b I drank the chocolate milkshake.

c Benji ran all the way home.

d Sasha yawned and lay down in bed.

e "I told you not to tell anyone!" said Anna.

3 Write a sentence about how you eat your breakfast in the morning. Use a strong adverb to make the sentence interesting.

Writing — Student's Book page 60

1 Read the first three paragraphs of the story *The New Boy* on page 60 of the Student's Book again. Write a different beginning to the story.

_____
_____
_____
_____
_____
_____
_____

2 Kate and Kamla take Amrik to visit another part of their city. What would they show him? What would he think? Write a short dialogue to describe this.

Remember! Use the correct punctuation.

_____
_____
_____
_____
_____
_____
_____
_____

Reading and writing Student's Book page 61

Read the text below. The writer has forgotten the paragraph breaks. Draw a mark like this // to show where the paragraphs need to go.

"Come on, Charlie," said Maya. "We're going to miss the bus!" "Hang on!" snapped Charlie. "Give me a moment – I'm nearly ready." "Well," said Maya, "I'm going to the bus stop. I'll see you there – if the bus doesn't get there before you do!" Maya skipped off down the road to the bus stop. Her friend Patsy was already waiting there. "Hi, Patsy!" yelled Maya. "Are you going to the match too?" "Of course!" said Patsy. "I wouldn't miss it – it's not every day that your team gets to the final!" Just then, Charlie came running up, panting and puffing. "I think you forgot something, Maya," he gasped. He was waving a pair of tickets for the match. "We won't get far without these!"

Spelling — Student's Book pages 61–62

1 The words in the box below all contain the letter string *ea*.
Write each word in the correct *ea* sound circle.

beach	dead	bread	breakfast	seat	deal	healthy
heal	meadow	steal	leaves	stealth	feast	feather
steam	reach	thread	team	bead	great	tread
spread	treat	peak	leather	break		

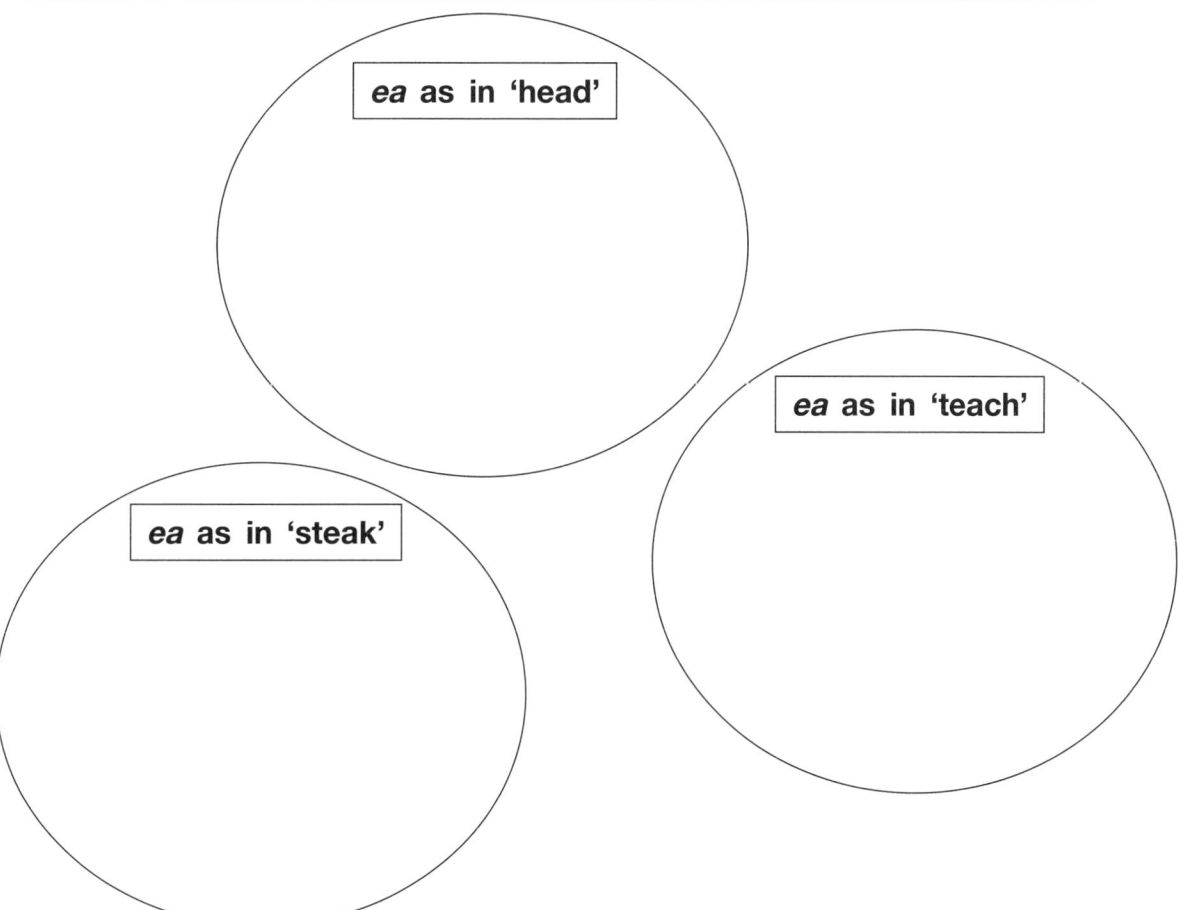

ea as in 'head'

ea as in 'teach'

ea as in 'steak'

2 Choose one word from each circle. Write a sentence using that word.

a *ea* as in 'head': _____

b *ea* as in 'steak': _____

c *ea* as in 'teach': _____

Writing Student's Book page 62

Read the sentences below. Write a more interesting word to replace the underlined word in each.

a   It was <u>great</u> when our team won the football match. _____

b   The flowers in Ravi's garden looked <u>nice</u>. _____

c   Maddie got lost in the <u>big</u> shop. _____

d   I saw a <u>little</u> mouse running across the floor. _____

e   Even though he was wearing his coat, Syed was <u>cold</u>. _____

f   Layla <u>shouted</u> to me across the crowded room. _____

g   Faraji <u>went</u> along the road. _____

h   I <u>like</u> chocolate cake. _____

i   I <u>hate</u> spinach. _____

j   The baby <u>cried</u> loudly. _____

6 Making the headlines

Reading and writing Student's Book pages 63–64

1 Reread the newspaper article *Malala's award*. Add notes to the spider diagram as you read.

Malala

2 Use your spider diagram to help you write a paragraph about Malala. Write at least one sentence for each point on your spider diagram.

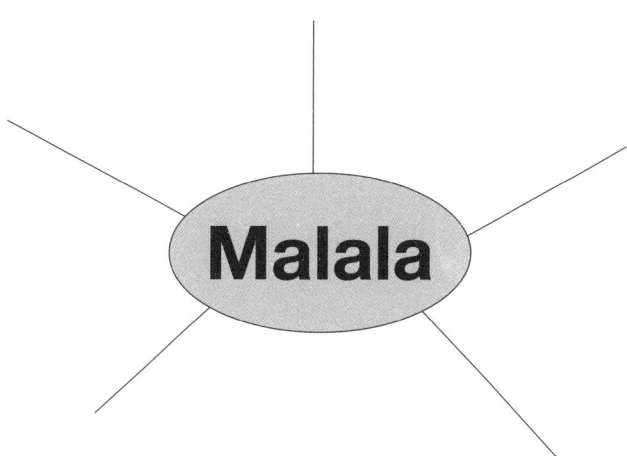

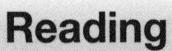

Reading — Student's Book page 64

1 Read the short newspaper article.

NEW FROG SPECIES FOUND

by Charles Matthews Science correspondent

June 2015: Brazilian scientists have discovered seven new species of tiny frogs, high up in the remote mountains on Brazil's southern coastline.

The new species have evolved with fewer fingers and toes than other frogs and they do not go through a tadpole stage. Instead, they come out of their eggs like fully-formed adults. They can even survive out of ponds and rivers because they are good at absorbing water from the ground through their skins. Most amazingly of all, the largest of the seven species grows to just 13 millimetres long!

Professor Marcio Pie, the lead scientist on the project, said that he had climbed more mountains than he can remember in search of the frogs. "It was really exhausting!" he told us. "But there was always the feeling of anticipation and curiosity about what the new species might look like."

2 Find the newspaper features below in the article.

- Draw a ring around the headline.
- Draw a wavy line under the journalist's name.
- Draw a straight line under the sentence that sums up the key point of the article.
- Draw a zigzag line under a sentence that grabs the reader's interest.
- Draw a dotted line under a quotation.

Spelling Student's Book page 65

1 Look at the root words below. Add *–ed* and *–ing* to each word.

a park   parked, parking

b dance   _____

c try   _____

d jog   _____

e step   _____

f stamp   _____

g carry   _____

h slope   _____

i glide   _____

j bury   _____

k dry   _____

l change   _____

m jump   _____

n pin   _____

2 Read the sentences below. Cross out any verbs that are spelled incorrectly. Write the correct spellings.

a Harry ~~walkied~~ slowly to school. walked

b I was hurriing so I triped up on the stairs. _____

c Selma placd her cup carefully on the table. _____

d Nadim had trouble liftying his heavy bag off the floor. _____

e My cousin is getting marryed next week. _____

f I voteed for Carlo to be Class President. _____

g My grandma knited me a purple and pink cardigan. _____

h We had fun slideing down the water slide. _____

Punctuation   Student's Book page 66

1 Add the missing commas to the sentences below.

a My dad goes out for a run every morning often as far as 10-kilometres.

b I nibbled on some delicious cookies even though Mum told me not to.

c Malala who is from Pakistan shared the prize with Kailash Satyarthi from India.

d Ali who does not like having a hair cut has hair dangling in his eyes.

e It was very cold almost freezing so I put on my thick coat.

2 Think of a phrase of your own to add between the commas in the sentences below. Say it out loud before you write it to make sure it makes sense.

a The children, _____ , played on the swings.

b Those cars, _____ , are very popular here.

c My favourite dinner, _____ , was waiting for me when I got home.

d My teacher Mrs Nosarka, _____ , gave us a Maths test.

e Mariam's best pen, _____ , seems to have gone missing.

Reading and writing Student's Book pages 72–73

1 Read the instructions a–f below. The connectives are missing. Choose the best connective from the box to fill each gap. You may need to use some more than once.

| first | next | and | so | then | finally | now |

Make a hoop game!

What you need:
- five paper plates
- the cardboard tube from a roll of kitchen paper
- a pencil
- a mug or glass
- a pair of scissors
- sticky tape
- brightly coloured paints or felt-tip pens

What to do:

a _____, take a paper plate _____ put the mug or glass down in the middle of it. Draw round the mug or glass _____ there is a circle in the middle of the plate.

b _____, cut the circle out of the middle of the plate _____ you are left with a ring.

c _____ do the same with three of the other plates.

d Colour or paint the rings using bright colours.

e _____, take the cardboard tube _____ stick it to the last plate with sticky tape, _____ it will stand upright.

f _____ throw your rings _____ see how many you can get to land over the tube!

2 Read the instructions above again. Draw a circle round all the command verbs (like 'make', 'do', and so on).

7 Inventions

Spelling Student's Book pages 77–78

1 Write the animal names below in alphabetical order.

> **Remember!**
> If there are two words starting with the same letters you need to look at the first different letters of each word to decide which comes first in the alphabet. For example:
> <u>k</u>angaroo
> <u>k</u>oala

kangaroo
elephant
lizard
mouse
hippopotamus
anteater
lion
rabbit
koala
elk
hare
antelope

2 Write the surnames below in alphabetical order.

Patel
Burroughs
Wang
Howard
Lau
Peters
Latimer
Bains
Smithson
Persaud
Khan
Hussain

_____
_____
_____
_____
_____
_____
_____
_____
_____
_____
_____
_____

3 The bands at a pop concert must perform in alphabetical order. The first group is called *Cutie*. Make up names for four other bands.

Remember that they need to be in alphabetical order.

Cutie _____ _____ _____ _____

Reading and writing Student's Book page 81

Read the letter your teacher will give you. Then answer the questions.

1 Write three reasons why *A. Baxter* thinks the internet is a great invention.

_____
_____
_____
_____

2 Why does *A. Baxter* think email is useful?

_____
_____

3 What was the date the letter was written?

_____
_____

4 Do you think *A. Baxter's* letter is convincing? Give a reason for your answer.

_____
_____

5 What do *you* think is the best invention ever? Explain why you think this. Give at least two reasons.

_____
_____
_____
_____

6 Find and write down three connectives used in the letter.

_____
_____

Verb tenses   Student's Book page 81

1 Change the sentences below to the past tense.

a   Orla will win the running race.
_____

b   I am glad to see Ella.
_____

2 Change the sentences below to the future tense.

a   We went to the beach on Saturday.
_____

b   They are painting Grace's bedroom pink.
_____

3 Change the sentences below to the present tense.

a   Janine will see the three kittens.
_____

b   Mum went to the shops.
_____

4 Read the story below. Draw a circle round sentences in the present tense. Draw a straight line under sentences in the past tense. Draw a wiggly line under sentences in the future tense.

It was Saturday afternoon and I was bored. Well, can you blame me? Nothing interesting will ever happen in our house. I had played all my games and read all my books, and I had nothing to do.

Suddenly there was a knock on my bedroom door. I got a shock!

"Who is that? What do you want?"

I crept to the door and opened it. You will never guess what I saw!

Punctuation Student's Book page 82

1 Add the correct punctuation to the end of each sentence below.

a I'm so glad you're coming round to our house to play
b Do you like chocolate
c It's my dad's birthday on Wednesday
d My teacher's name is Mrs Ismael
e There's a wasp on your arm
f I've never felt so happy
g There's a dragon in the playground
h How many sisters do you have
i Dad's favourite colour is green
j On Saturday we went to the shops

Remember!

Use the correct punctuation at the end of each sentence.

2 Write a question, an exclamation and a statement.

- Question: _____

- Exclamation: _____

- Statement: _____

Spelling — Student's Book page 85

1 Draw lines to link the nouns with the verbs they come from.

excitement	operate
celebration	decide
management	divert
connection	excite
agreement	define
decision	celebrate
definition	manage
argument	educate
diversion	measure
measurement	connect
education	agree
operation	argue

2 Write the verb that each of the nouns below comes from.

a   announcement   _____

b   contradiction   _____

c   punishment   _____

d   demonstration   _____

e   entertainment   _____

f   co-operation   _____

g   encouragement   _____

3 **Write the noun that comes from the verbs below.**

a decorate _____

b possess _____

c assess _____

d navigate _____

e pay _____

f irritate _____

g announce _____

Remember!
The nouns end in either *–ion* or *–ment*.

4 **Make as many words as you can with the letters in the puzzle below.**

- Use the middle letter (i) in all of the words you make.
- All the words should have at least three letters.
- There is a nine letter word hidden in the grid. See if you can find it.

e	o	p
a	i	n
t	r	o

_____ _____ _____
_____ _____ _____
_____ _____ _____
_____ _____ _____

8 Putting on a show

Verbs and adverbs Student's Book page 92

1 Read the sentences below. Draw a circle round the powerful verbs.

a   Li-Wei stomped crossly out of the room.

b   Maxine grabbed the plate and hurled it out of the window.

c   "How dare you do that?" Mum thundered.

d   Romy's cat Alexia slunk in through the door.

e   "It wasn't my fault," muttered Sam.

f   The hippopotamus wallowed in the soft river mud.

g   Eight pigeons strutted towards us, looking for food.

h   I yelled at my brother because he used my pens without asking.

2 Add adverbs (like 'sadly' or 'happily') in the brackets below to show how the character would say the words.

a   **ALICE:** (_____) I can't believe you just did that!

b   **MUM:** (_____) Never mind darling. It'll all be over soon.

c   **GRAN:** (_____) Well in my day children had to play quietly!

d   **MR ABAJO:** (_____) Class Four! Come back here this instant!

e   **ASIF:** (_____) I wish we could go to Fab Towers theme park!

f   **BARNEY:** (_____) I'm only coming if Jake can come too.

g   **FATIMA:** (_____) Oh! I didn't see you standing there Selma!

h   **DAD:** (_____) Hurry up, boys! You'll be late for school!

Spelling Student's Book page 94

1 Add *im–*, *in–*, *ir–* or *il–* to the words in the box to make the opposite meaning.

> _____visible   _____logical   _____credible   _____possible
>
> _____relevant   _____mature   _____correct

2 Now use the new words to complete the crossword below.

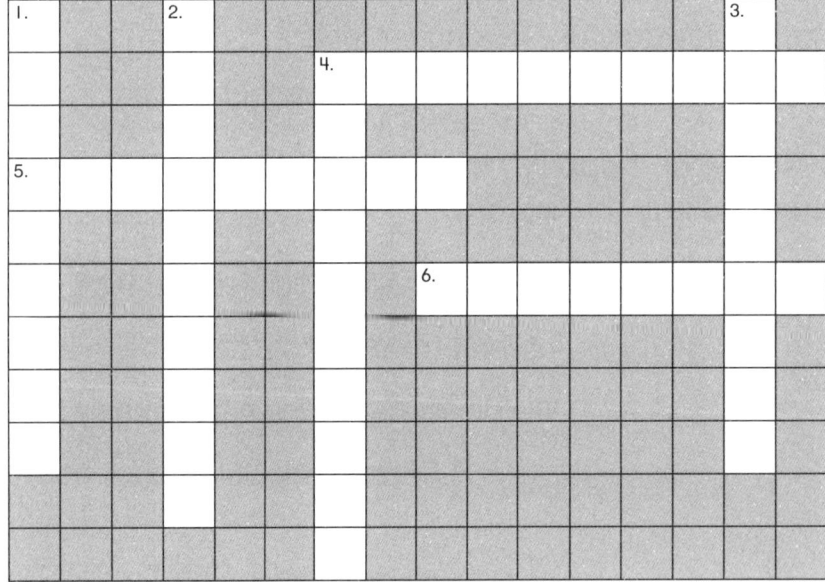

Clues

Down
1 You can't see it.
2 It just can't be done.
3 It's not right.
4 I don't believe it!

Across
4 That's nothing to do with it – it's _____.
5 There's no logic to that!
6 Act your age – you're so _____!

Spelling — Student's Book page 95

Write the plural forms of the words in brackets to complete each sentence correctly.

a They took down all the (shelf) _____ in the living room to look for the mouse.

b Peter, the cat and the bird were sitting up in the (branch) _____ of a big tree.

c Are there any (wolf) _____ in this forest?

d I enjoy reading (diary) _____ because they tell us about real events and how people felt about them.

e Who are the main (character) _____ in this play?

Vocabulary — Student's Book page 95

1 Read the sentences below. Find a synonym in the box that you could use for each underlined word. You can use words from the box or you can use other words that you know.

> cross   sing   staggered   hung   danced

a The birds chirp early in the morning. _____

b The hippo waddled down to the river and started to swim. _____

c He skipped along the path happily. _____

d My sister was so angry when we played a trick on her. _____

e Peter dangled a rope from the tree. _____

2 Write out the words in the box in the order you would find them in the dictionary. Then write a definition of each word. Use your dictionary if you need to.

anger	bath	angrily	balance	submarine
subtle	brim	beetle	alligator	seahorse
seaside	trainers	flying	triangle	fairground
triple	valiant	valuable		

Word: _____ Definition: _____

Word: _____ Definition: _____

Word: _____ Definition: _____

Word: _____ Definition: _____

Word: _____ Definition: _____

Word: _____ Definition: _____

Word: _____ Definition: _____

Word: _____ Definition: _____

Word: _____ Definition: _____

Word: _____ Definition: _____

Word: _____ Definition: _____

Word: _____ Definition: _____

Word: _____ Definition: _____

Word: _____ Definition: _____

Word: _____ Definition: _____

Word: _____ Definition: _____

Word: _____ Definition: _____

Word: _____ Definition: _____

9 Imaginary worlds

Reading and speaking   Student's Book pages 98–99

Read the words in the box below. Add each of the words to the correct list.

scientist	walk	guess	scenic	scent	lamb	debt
foreign	knew	resign	chalk	knife	scenery	kneel
hymn	crumb	know	solemn	listen	campaign	
jostle	talk	wriggle	rustle	wrinkle	thistle	disguise
guest	wrap	knot	wreckage	half	comb	calf

Silent c
science
scene
ascend
_____
_____
_____
_____

Silent b
doubt
bomb
_____
_____
_____
_____

Silent g
sign
gnome
gnat
_____
_____
_____
_____

Silent k
knight
knee
_____
_____
_____
_____
_____

Silent n
autumn
column
_____
_____
_____
_____

Silent w
wreck
wrong
_____
_____
_____
_____

Silent t
bristle
castle
_____
_____
_____
_____

Silent u
guitar
guilty
_____
_____
_____
_____

Silent l
calm
balm
_____
_____
_____
_____

Verb tenses Student's Book page 100

1 Underline the verbs in the dialogues below. At the end of each sentence, write 'past', 'present' or 'future'.

a "I am going to count up to ten, and then I will come and find you!" _____

b "How many biscuits did you eat?" _____

c "It is Dad's turn to cook dinner today." _____

d "Gran said I could take Fluffy for a walk." _____

e "My favourite colour is red." _____

f "We are going to go to America on holiday next year." _____

2 Add the missing verbs to the dialogues below.

a "Molly <u>is going to</u> come round to my house today." (future)

b "We _____ down to the park after school." (future)

c "I hope there _____ pasta for tea." (future)

d "Kenzie _____ the winner of the running race." (past)

e "When I _____ little, my favourite toy _____ a bear." (past)

f "We _____ a big chocolate cake on my birthday." (past)

g "_____ you ready to go out?" (present)

h "Mum _____ calling you!" (present)

i "My favourite team _____ Real Madrid." (present)

Verbs and adverbs — Student's Book page 102

1 Replace the verbs in the story below with more interesting verbs. Cross out the verbs and write a more exciting verb above each one.

Jamie went down from the spaceship on to the planet surface. He looked around him. When he saw a herd of big aliens coming towards him he shouted out. He went back to the spaceship but it was too late. The aliens had seen him and they went towards the spaceship.

2 Add some interesting adverbs to the sentences below.

a   The aliens flew _____ across the desert towards us.

b   Their eyes glinted _____ in the light of the fire.

c   The space monster roared _____ .

d   The captain shouted at us _____ .

3 Add some interesting descriptive adjectives to the sentences below.

a   The herd of _____ aliens was thundering towards Jamie.

b   Their _____ mouths were full of _____ teeth.

c   Jamie could see their _____ claws reaching out towards him.

Punctuation

Student's Book pages 107–108

1 Add the missing punctuation to the dialogues below.

a Are you ready to land on the planet surface asked the Captain

b Yes said Jenna I think I'm as ready as I'll ever be

c Good said the captain This is going to be a very difficult mission

d I'm sure I'm ready for it said Jenna

e Don't forget your invisibility shield said the Captain You're going to need it

2 Imagine that when Jenna lands on the planet she finds a nest of alien dinosaurs. They are only babies, but they are huge. Then she hears a rumbling sound and looks up. The babies' mother is running towards her!

Write the conversation she has with the Captain when she radios back to the spaceship for help. Write at least two things for each character to say. Remember to use punctuation.

Jenna: _____

_____

Captain: _____

_____

Jenna: _____

_____

Captain: _____

_____

Writing Student's Book page 105

1 **Fill in the boxes below to help you plan a non-rhyming poem about an imaginary creature.**

What kind of creature will you write about? It could be an imaginary creature you have read about (like an ogre, a dragon or an elf) or it could be one you have made up yourself.

Write the creature's name here.

_____

It looks like ...	It sounds like ...

It moves like ...	It makes me feel ...

2 What does the creature do? Write some notes below about what might happen in the poem.

> First the creature …
>
> Then it …
>
> At the end of the poem it …

3 Can you think of any similes (like 'as dark as night') to describe your creature? Write them below.

4 Can you think of an interesting word or phrase that would make a good repeating phrase for your poem? Write it below.

5 Now write a first draft of your poem. The way a poem sounds is very important. Say the words out loud to yourself to make sure that they sound good.

6 Make any changes you need to and then write out the whole poem in your best handwriting. You could add a drawing of your imaginary creature.

Homophones Student's Book page 106

1 Read the sentences below. Underline the homophones.

a I have something in my eye.
b My dad says my brother has a hole in his stomach. He ate the whole cake.
c Have you met Yuki and Jen? They're from Japan and this is their house.
d We waited at the station for two hours, from four o'clock until six o'clock.
e Look at all of ships out at sea today. How many can you see?
f There are too many cars on the road and they all seem to be going to the same place.

2 Draw a line between the homophone pairs below.

eye	wear
bear	there
by	write
deer	hole
four	buy
hour	I
whole	our
male	one
won	some
right	sea
see	bare
sum	dear
their	for
too	mail
where	two

3 **Choose the correct homophone from the lists on page 59 to fill each of the gaps in the sentences.**

a _____ are you going?

b I left my bag over _____.

c Lara can _____ very neatly.

d Our team _____ the obstacle race.

e We've got chicken noodle soup _____ dinner.

f The postman has just delivered the _____.

g Would you like _____ juice?

h The little boat was floating on the _____.

i I finished reading the _____ book in one day.

j I went to the park and Ahmed came _____.